HAL•LEONARD
INSTRUMENTAL
PLAY-ALONG

VIOLA

WEST SIDE STORY®

Based on a conception of Jerome Robbins

Book by

Arthur Laurents

Music by

Leonard Bernstein®

Lyrics by

Stephen Sondheim

Entire Original Production
Directed and Choreographed by

Jerome Robbi[ns]

ISBN 978-1-4234-5831-9

LEONARD
BERNSTEIN
Music Publishing
Company LLC

BOOSEY & HAWKES

AN IMAGEM COMPANY

DISTRIBUTED BY

HAL•LEONARD®
CORPORATION
7777 W. BLUEMOUND RD. P.O. BOX 13819 MILWAUKEE, WI 53213

Visit Hal Leonard Online at
www.halleonard.com

TITLE	PAGE	CD TRACK
America	3	1
Cool	4	2
I Feel Pretty	5	3
I Have a Love	6	4
Jet Song	7	5
Maria	8	6
One Hand, One Heart	9	7
Something's Coming	10	8
Somewhere	12	9
Tonight	13	10
A Tuning Notes		11

How To Use The CD Accompaniment:
A melody cue appears on the right channel only. If your CD player has a balance adjustment, you can adjust the volume of the melody by turning down the right channel.

The CD is playable on any CD player, and is also enhanced so PC and MAC users can adjust the recording to any tempo without changing the pitch.

◆ AMERICA

Lyrics by STEPHEN SONDHEIM
Music by LEONARD BERNSTEIN

VIOLA

② COOL

Lyrics by STEPHEN SONDHEIM
Music by LEONARD BERNSTEIN

VIOLA

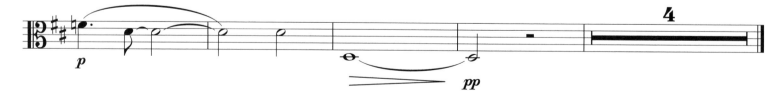

❸ I FEEL PRETTY

VIOLA

Lyrics by STEPHEN SONDHEIM
Music by LEONARD BERNSTEIN

◆ I HAVE A LOVE

VIOLA

Lyrics by STEPHEN SONDHEIM
Music by LEONARD BERNSTEIN

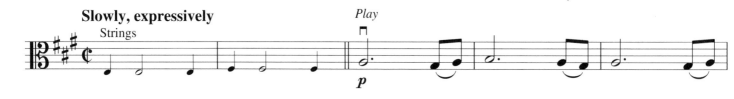

◆ JET SONG

VIOLA

Lyrics by STEPHEN SONDHEIM
Music by LEONARD BERNSTEIN

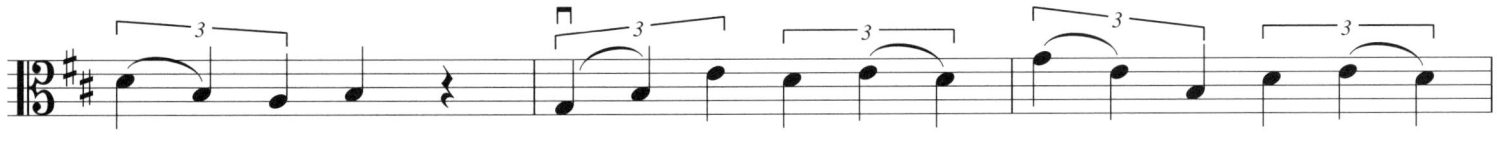

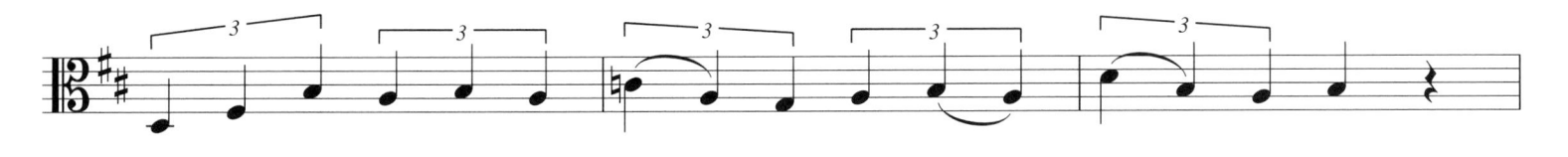

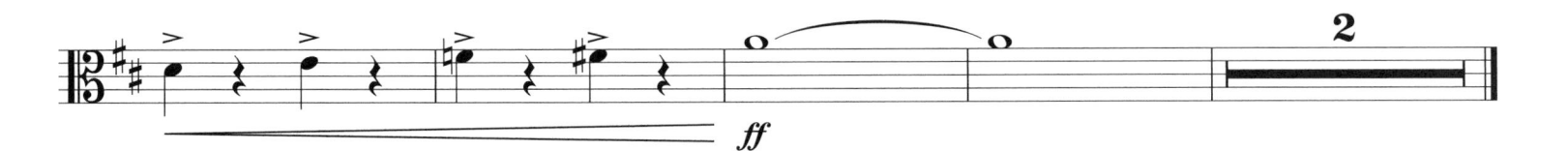

◆ MARIA

VIOLA

Lyrics by STEPHEN SONDHEIM
Music by LEONARD BERNSTEIN

Lyrical, with feeling

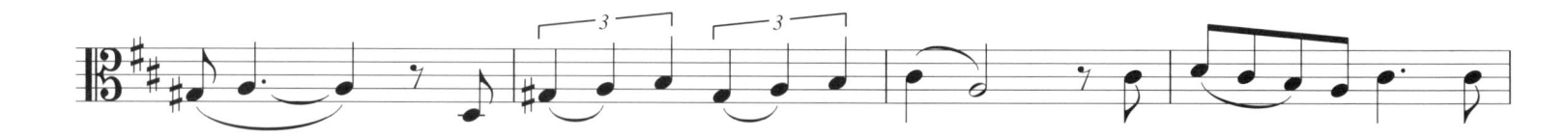

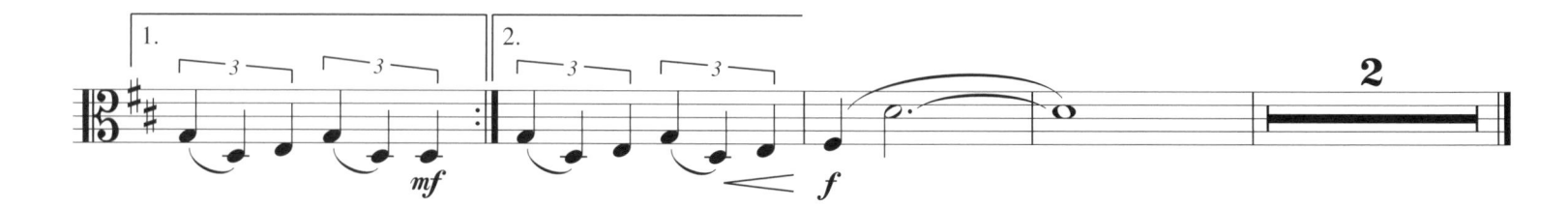

7 ONE HAND, ONE HEART

VIOLA

Lyrics by STEPHEN SONDHEIM
Music by LEONARD BERNSTEIN

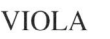

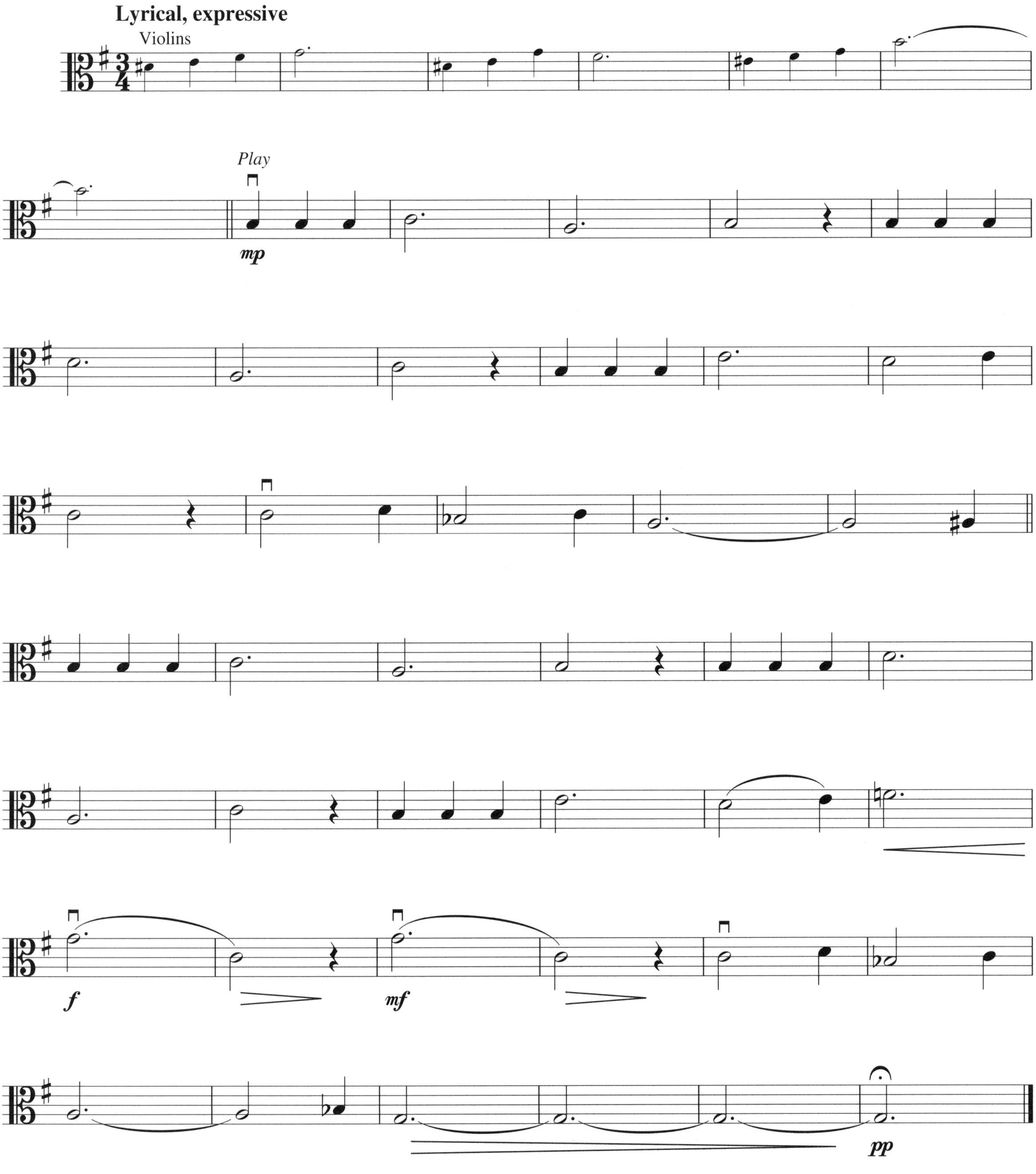

 SOMETHING'S COMING

VIOLA

Lyrics by STEPHEN SONDHEIM
Music by LEONARD BERNSTEIN

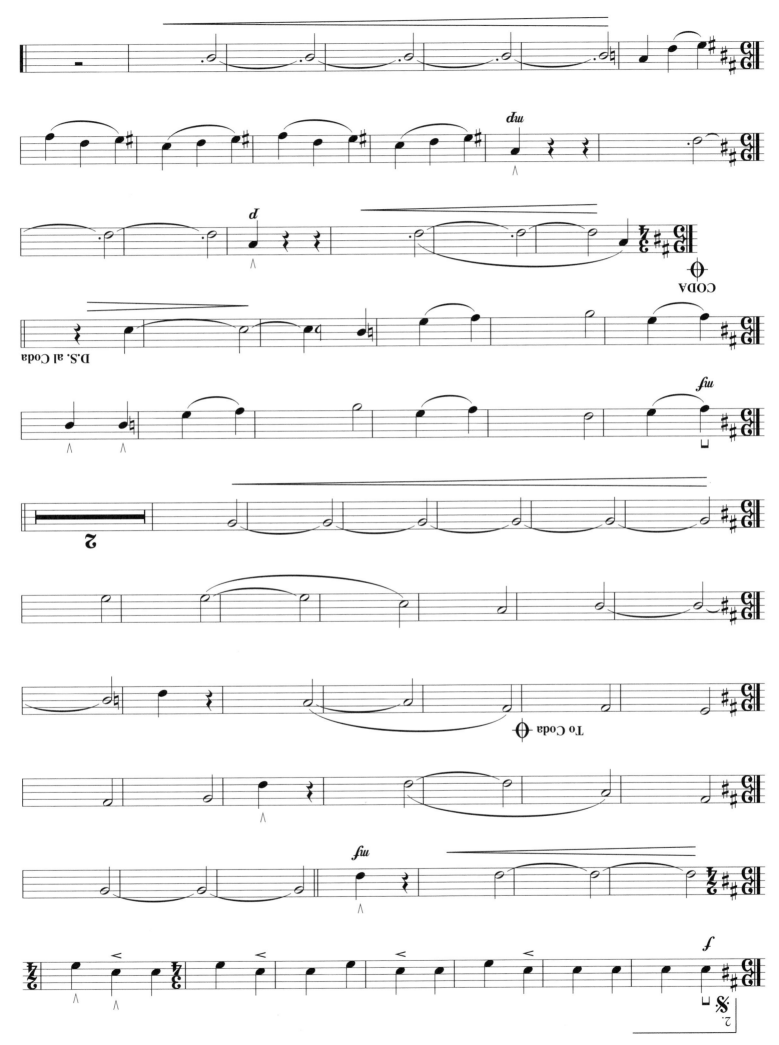

11

SOMEWHERE

VIOLA

Lyrics by STEPHEN SONDHEIM
Music by LEONARD BERNSTEIN

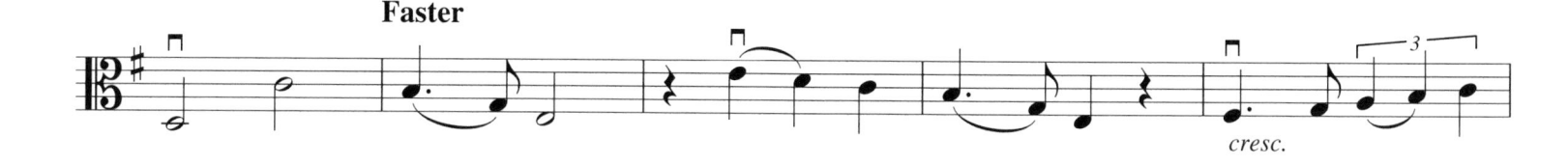

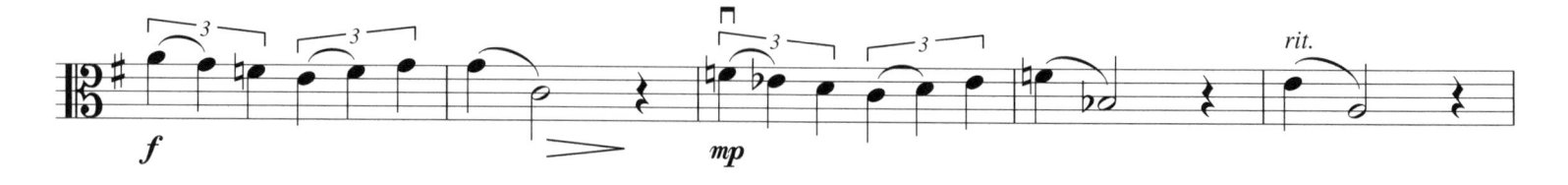

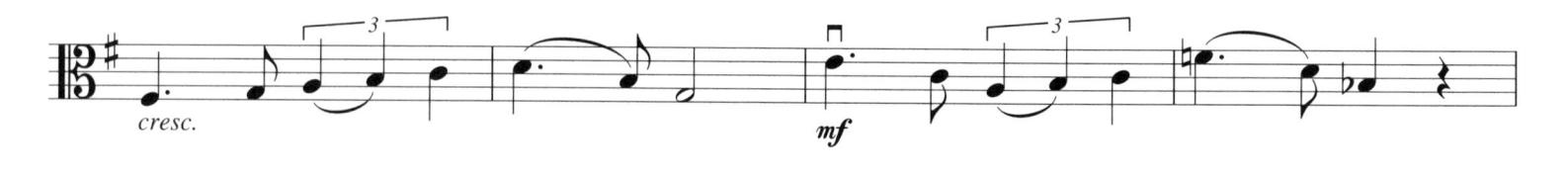

◆ TONIGHT

VIOLA

Lyrics by STEPHEN SONDHEIM
Music by LEONARD BERNSTEIN